Rihanna

ABDO
Publishing Company

Big Buddy BOOKS
Buddy Bios

by Sarah Tieck

VISIT US AT

www.abdopublishing.com

Published by ABDO Publishing Company, PO Box 398166, Minneapolis, MN 55439.

Printed in the United States of America, North Mankato, Minnesota.
102011
012012

♺ PRINTED ON RECYCLED PAPER

Coordinating Series Editor: Rochelle Baltzer
Contributing Editors: Megan M. Gunderson, BreAnn Rumsch, Marcia Zappa
Graphic Design: Maria Hosley
Cover Photograph: *AP Photo*: Gregg DeGuire/PictureGroup via AP IMAGES.
Interior Photographs/Illustrations: *AP Photo*: Evan Agostini (p. 25), Vince Bucci/PictureGroup via AP IMAGES
    (p. 21), Kristie Bull/Graylock.com (p. 13), Jeff Daly/PictureGroup via AP IMAGES (p. 23), Gregg DeGuire/
    PictureGroup via AP IMAGES (p. 27), Kevork Djansezian (p. 17), Louis Lanzano (p. 13), Press Association via
    AP Images (p. 29), Mark J. Terrill (pp. 15, 17), M. Vaudrey/PictureGroup via AP IMAGES (p. 4); *Getty Images*:
    Brian Ach (p. 26), Ida Mae Astute/ABC via Getty Images (p. 19), Scott Gries/Getty Images for Universal Magic
    (p. 9), John Rocal/NY Daily News Archive via Getty Images (p. 11), Michael Tran/FilmMagic (p. 7); *Shutterstock*:
    Mindy w.m. Chung (p. 9), Fairy Lens (p. 9).

Library of Congress Cataloging-in-Publication Data

Tieck, Sarah, 1976-
  Rihanna : singing sensation / Sarah Tieck.
    p. cm. -- (Big buddy biographies)
  ISBN 978-1-61783-228-4
  1. Rihanna, 1988---Juvenile literature. 2. Singers--Biography--Juvenile literature. I. Title.
  ML3930.R44T54 2012
  782.42164092--dc23
  [B]
                              2011037822

Contents

Rihanna often performs live. She says she shares her feelings through her music.

Music Star

Rihanna is a talented singer. She is best known for singing popular music. Her albums and songs are well liked around the world.

Where in the World?

MARTINIQUE
(FRANCE)

ATLANTIC
OCEAN

SAINT LUCIA

CARIBBEAN SEA

SAINT VINCENT AND
THE GRENADINES

BARBADOS

Saint Michael

N
W E
S

Family Ties

Rihanna's real name is Robyn Rihanna Fenty. She was born in Saint Michael **parish**, Barbados, on February 20, 1988. Her parents are Ronald and Monica Fenty. Rihanna has two younger brothers named Rorrey and Rajad.

While Rihanna was growing up, her mom was a businesswoman. Her dad worked in a warehouse. When Rihanna was a teenager, her parents got a divorce.

Young Rihanna was a tomboy. Sometimes, she even wore clothes that belonged to her brothers! She changed her look when she became a singer.

Island Life

Rihanna grew up in the country of Barbados. Nearly 300,000 people live on this island. Palm trees, beaches, and warm weather make Barbados a popular vacation spot.

Today, Rihanna makes music in the United States. But, she often returns to her home country. She visits the beach with family and friends. There, they play games and swim in the ocean!

Barbados has flowers almost all year long! The national flower is called Pride of Barbados. It grows all over the island.

The capital of Barbados is Bridgetown. It has many shops and businesses as well as a busy harbor.

In 2006, Rihanna gave a special performance in Barbados.

Starting Out

Growing up, Rihanna sang for fun whenever she could. She even pretended her brush was a microphone! Around 2002, she formed a singing group with some friends.

In 2003, Rihanna sang for a music **producer**. He liked her voice and thought she could be a successful singer. So, she moved to the United States and made a **demo**.

Rapper and music **executive** Jay-Z heard Rihanna's demo. He offered her a record contract. Soon, Rihanna began working on her first album.

Jay-Z's popularity helped Rihanna find success quickly.

When Rihanna released her first album, very few people knew of her. She worked hard to gain fans.

In 2005, Rihanna **released** her first album. For *Music of the Sun*, she mixed Caribbean music with **rhythm and blues**. The album sold many copies in the United States. Its first hit song was "Pon de Replay."

Right away, Rihanna began recording more songs. In 2006, she released *A Girl Like Me*. Her second album did even better! Rihanna was becoming a star.

About three months after it came out, *A Girl Like Me* went platinum. That means it sold more than 1 million copies!

Rising Star

For her third album, Rihanna cut her hair and changed her look. *Good Girl Gone Bad* came out in 2007.

One song from the album was **released** early. "Umbrella" features a **rap** by Jay-Z. It quickly became a number one hit!

Did you know...

Rihanna often changes her fashion style, including her hair. This helps her stand out!

Good Girl Gone Bad had seven hit songs! These included "Shut Up and Drive" and "Disturbia."

"Umbrella" proved to be an especially important song for Rihanna. In 2008, she received her first Grammy Award for her work on it!

Rihanna and Jay-Z won the Grammy together for "Umbrella."

Life Changes

Rihanna was planning to **perform** at the 2009 Grammy Awards. Then, her life changed. Rihanna and her boyfriend had an argument, and he hurt her.

Rihanna cancelled her Grammy performance. But, she didn't hide what happened. Over time, she shared her story. She ended her relationship. Rihanna's actions helped many people learn that it is not okay to hurt others.

Rihanna shared her story on television. She said, "This happened to me...it can happen to anyone."

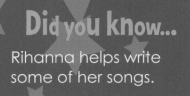
A New Day

Rihanna took some time away from music to heal. Later in 2009, she **released** her fourth album. It is called *Rated R*. She changed her look again, and some people said the album had an angry sound.

In 2010, Rihanna's fifth album came out. It is called *Loud*. Some of its songs became hits, including "Only Girl (In the World)."

Rihanna sang "Love the Way You Lie" with rapper Eminem for his 2010 album. The song was about couples who hurt each other. It brought awareness to this problem.

A Singer's Life

Rihanna works hard on her music. She spends many hours recording albums. After an album is **released**, Rihanna goes on concert tours. Her shows include singing and dancing. So, Rihanna must help plan and practice before **performing**.

Rihanna's concerts often feature colorful costumes!

When she is on tour, Rihanna may spend months away from home. She travels to cities around the world and **performs** live concerts. She also attends events and meets fans. Her fans are always excited to see her!

Many Rihanna fans are part of a group called the Rihanna Navy. They support her music.

Off the Stage

Rihanna has a pet dog. It is a maltipoo.

When Rihanna has free time, she visits friends and family in the United States and Barbados. She also likes to help people and work with **charities**.

Rihanna is especially interested in helping children. In 2006, she created the Believe Foundation. It provides health care, school supplies, clothes, and toys to sick and poor children worldwide.

In 2011, Rihanna released a perfume. It is called Reb'l Fleur.

Buzz

Rihanna's opportunities continue to grow. In late 2011, she **released** her sixth album. It is called *Talk That Talk*. She also hopes to attend college one day.

Fans are excited to see what's next for Rihanna. Many believe she has a bright **future**!

Reporters often take Rihanna's picture. And, fans ask for her autograph.

Snapshot

★**Name**: Robyn Rihanna Fenty

★**Birthday**: February 20, 1988

★**Birthplace**: Saint Michael parish, Barbados

★**Albums**: *Music of the Sun, A Girl Like Me, Good Girl Gone Bad, Rated R, Loud, Talk That Talk*

Important Words

charity a group or a fund that helps people in need.

demo a recording to show a musical group or artist's abilities.

executive (ihg-ZEH-kyuh-tihv) a high-level employee who manages or directs a company.

future (FYOO-chuhr) a time that has not yet occurred.

parish a small area that has its own government.

perform to do something in front of an audience.

producer a person who oversees the making of a movie, a play, an album, or a radio or television show.

rap a type of music in which the words of a song are spoken to a beat. A rapper is someone who raps.

release to make available to the public.

rhythm (RIH-thuhm) **and blues** a form of popular music that features a strong beat. It is inspired by jazz, gospel, and blues styles.

Web Sites

To learn more about Rihanna, visit ABDO Publishing Company online. Web sites about Rihanna are featured on our Book Links page. These links are routinely monitored and updated to provide the most current information available.

www.abdopublishing.com

Index